NATIONAL GEOGRAPHIC

Ladders

AMAZING PLANTS

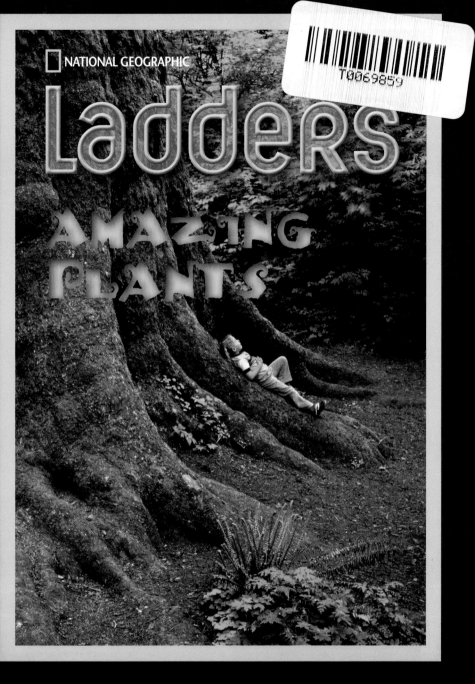

The King's Tree 2
   retold by Elizabeth Gilbert
   illustrated by Karla Diaz Castro

Extreme Plants 8
   by Jennifer Boudart

The Plant Hunt 18
   by Renee Biermann
   illustrated by C. B. Canga

Discuss 32

IN THE MIDDLE OF THE NIGHT, PADMA SAID GOODBYE TO HER SLEEPING HUSBAND.

SHE SNEAKED OUT TO THE PEACEFUL WATER GARDEN BEHIND THE PALACE.

PADMA JUMPED INTO THE SHALLOW POOL IN THE GARDEN AND CHANGED INTO A LOTUS FLOWER.

THE NEXT MORNING, THE KING AWOKE WITH A FEELING THAT SOMETHING WAS TERRIBLY WRONG. HE DECIDED HE MUST FIND PADMA RIGHT AWAY.

THE KING ORDERED EVERYONE TO SEARCH THE PALACE AND ITS GROUNDS, BUT PADMA WAS NOWHERE TO BE FOUND.

AFTER ALMOST GIVING UP HOPE, THE KING FOUND HIMSELF AT THE WATER GARDEN. THERE HE SAW THE LOTUS FLOWER IN ITS WATERY **HABITAT.**

FROM WHERE CAME THIS BEAUTIFUL FLOWER? IT BRINGS ME JOY, AS IF I WERE SEEING PADMA HERSELF.

I SHALL VISIT ITS LOVELY PETALS EVERY DAY!

I MUST DESTROY THAT UGLY FLOWER!

AFTER THE KING HAD GONE, DREADED WITCH CAST A SPELL ON THE POOL, DRAINING ITS WATER.

THEN SHE CAST ANOTHER SPELL, WHICH CAUSED THE FLOWER TO BURST INTO FLAMES, LEAVING ONLY ASHES.

LATER THAT NIGHT . . .

A TINY PLANT SPROUTED FROM THE FLOWER'S ASHES.

THE SPROUT GREW TALLER AND TALLER.

FROM THE LOTUS ASHES GREW THE FIRST MANGO TREE. IT WAS **BLOOMING** WITH HUNDREDS OF FLOWERS.

YESTERDAY, THIS POOL WAS FULL OF WATER. WITHIN THE POOL BLOOMED ONE BEAUTIFUL LOTUS FLOWER.

IN THIS CHANGED HABITAT STANDS A KIND OF TREE I'VE NEVER SEEN. YET THE TREE HAS **ADAPTATIONS** THAT MAKE IT PERFECT FOR THIS PLACE.

IT HAS NOT ONE FLOWER, BUT HUNDREDS!

ONE DAY, WHEN THE KING VISITED THE MANGO TREE, HE NOTICED FRUIT GROWING FROM ITS BRANCHES.

THE FRUIT BEGAN TO **RIPEN.**

THE KING SMELLED THE RIPENED FRUIT. IT SMELLED SWEET AND DELICIOUS.

HUH?

THE FRUIT BEGAN TO GROW. IT GREW UNTIL IT BURST.

PADMA, YOU HAVE COME BACK!

I HAVE NOT LEFT YOU, NOR HAVE YOU LEFT ME. HAPPINESS AND LOVE CAN CHANGE. BUT THEY CAN NEVER BE DESTROYED.

BEFORE DREADED WITCH FLED THE KINGDOM, SHE CAST ONE LAST SPELL. SHE WANTED TO REMIND PEOPLE THAT HAPPINESS DOES NOT ALWAYS COME EASILY. FROM THEN ON, THE SKIN OF THE MANGO HAS BEEN TOUGH. IT MUST BE CUT BEFORE ONE CAN ENJOY THE SWEETNESS INSIDE.

Check In What plants did Padma change into?

Extreme Plants

by Jennifer Boudart

Plants live in almost every kind of **habitat** on Earth. They grow down low, in ponds and marshes. They grow up high, along mountain ridges. Plants even grow in harsh habitats, such as burning deserts and freezing tundra. Plants have **adaptations** that help them survive in their environment. The way plants look and grow helps them survive. The following plants have extreme adaptations.

The Biggest Bloomer!

The rafflesia is a jungle plant in Southeast Asia. It produces a single, huge flower. This flower grows up to 1 meter (about 3 feet) across and weighs up to 7 kilograms (15 pounds). The **bloom** smells like rotting meat! The awful smell attracts flies that eat dead animals. The flies pick up pollen as they crawl on the flower. When they fly to another stinky bloom, they spread the pollen. Pollen must be moved between plants for the plants to reproduce.

The rafflesia's bloom is the largest in the world.

A Green Giant!

The giant sequoia lives up to its name. This tree is the biggest plant **species** on Earth because of its mass, or bulk. The giant sequoia's trunk makes up most of its mass. The trunk on a full-grown tree is usually more than 6 meters (20 feet) across. Giant sequoias are tall, too. They are often 76 meters (about 250 feet) tall. A few are more than 93 meters (305 feet). That's taller than the Statue of Liberty!

To see the giant sequoias, you have to visit the Sierra Nevada in eastern California.

Many giant sequoias have survived more than 3,000 years. What adaptations help giant sequoias live so long? Their bark protects the tree from disease. Also, giant sequoias can grow new bark quickly to cover burns from forest fires. When a fully grown giant sequoia dies, it's usually because the tree fell over. This happens after the soil is no longer able to hold the tree's roots.

The most massive giant sequoia is named the General Sherman Tree. This tree stands about 84 meters (275 feet) tall. Its trunk measures 11 meters (35 feet) across! The General Sherman could supply enough wood to build 40 houses. Luckily it is illegal to cut down giant sequoias.

Statue of Liberty	General Sherman	U.S. Capitol building
93 meters	84 meters	88 meters
(305 feet)	(275 feet)	(288 feet)

This is King Clone, the oldest known creosote bush. It forms a ring about 14 meters (45 feet) across. Scientists think King Clone first sprouted from a seed 13,700 years ago!

Blast from the Past!

The creosote bush grows in the deserts of North America. It looks like a ring of bushes growing around an empty center. It is among the longest-living plants on Earth.

The creosote bush starts out as one parent plant, which can live 200 years. During that time, the parent plant sends out shoots all around it. Each shoot grows into a new bush, which is an exact copy

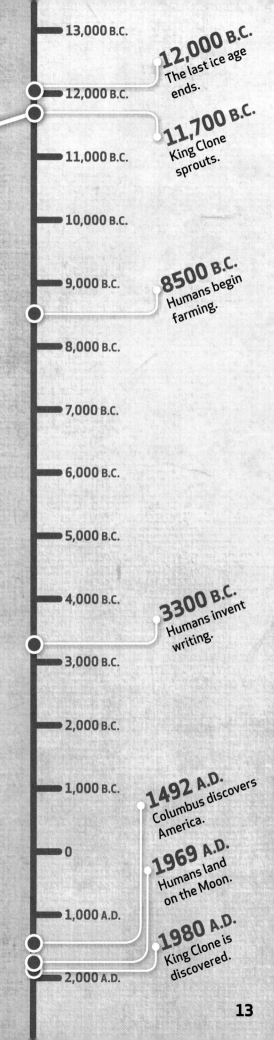

13,000 B.C.

12,000 B.C.
The last ice age ends.

12,000 B.C.

11,700 B.C.
King Clone sprouts.

11,000 B.C.

10,000 B.C.

8500 B.C.
Humans begin farming.

9,000 B.C.

8,000 B.C.

7,000 B.C.

6,000 B.C.

5,000 B.C.

4,000 B.C.

3300 B.C.
Humans invent writing.

3,000 B.C.

2,000 B.C.

1,000 B.C.

1492 A.D.
Columbus discovers America.

0

1969 A.D.
Humans land on the Moon.

1,000 A.D.

1980 A.D.
King Clone is discovered.

2,000 A.D.

of the parent plant. And each new bush does the same as its parent. It sends out shoots and makes new copies of itself. Over time, the parent plant dies. But a ring of "daughter" plants is left behind. The parent plant "lives on" because it has made copies of itself. In this way, some creosote bushes have lived for thousands of years.

A Turbo Grower!

Bamboo grows well in East and Southeast Asia, where the climate is wet and warm. Some species of bamboo may be the fastest-growing plants on Earth.

Bamboos are grasses, but they look more like trees. They have a woody stem and leafy branches. Like trees, some grow very tall. A few species of bamboo reach 40 meters (about 130 feet) or more. Unlike trees, bamboo can grow very quickly. Some may grow 2.5 centimeters (1 inch) per hour. Imagine if the grass in people's lawns grew that fast!

Node
The nodes look like rings. The stem is hollow except at each node. Leaves and branches sprout from nodes.

Culm
The culm is the bamboo's stem. The culm is mostly hollow, yet its wood is very strong.

Internode
Internodes are the hollow sections between nodes.

Rhizome
The rhizome is an underground stem.

Roots

People use bamboo in thousands of ways. The seeds and shoots can be eaten. Its sturdy wood can be used to make furniture, musical instruments, and homes. How are these people using bamboo?

A bamboo forest near Kyoto, Japan

A Microgreen!

Watermeal is the world's smallest flowering plant species. One watermeal plant is less than a millimeter long. It's no bigger than a small grain of sand. A dozen of the plant's blooms could fit on the head of a pin! Watermeal does not have roots or stems. Its tiny size and rounded form are adaptations that help it float in large numbers on lakes, ponds, marshes, and streams.

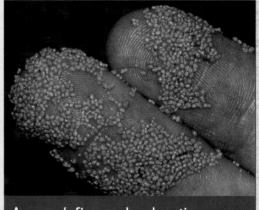

A person's fingers show how tiny watermeal plants are.

A giant Amazon water lily can easily support 23 kilograms (50 pounds).

A Leaf Beyond Belief!

Do you think only frogs can float on lily pads? Think again! A giant Amazon water lily can hold the weight of people without sinking. Its leaves stretch 2.5 meters (8 feet) across. This plant's adaptations help it float. The weight of its wide, flat leaves is spread out. Air fills its veins to help the leaves float. Spines on the bottom of each leaf protect it from hungry fish. Notches along the edges help water drain off, so the leaf doesn't fill and sink.

Some plant species have developed extreme adaptations. Do any extreme plants grow where you live?

This giant Amazon water lily can hold three people.

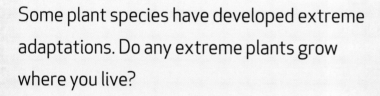

Check In Which extreme plants can live for longer than 3,000 years?

The Plant Hunt

by Renee Biermann
illustrated by C. B. Canga

NARRATOR

MRS. BLANKENSHIP
female teacher

INTRODUCTION

[**SETTING** *The play takes place at City Botanical Gardens. NARRATOR enters and speaks to the audience.*]

NARRATOR: Welcome to City Botanical Gardens! Mrs. Blankenship has brought a special group of students to this indoor **habitat** for a scavenger hunt. She has given them a Scavenger Hunt Notebook, a measuring tape, and gardening gloves. They are going to hunt for five unusual plants. How will they locate these mysterious plants? And what will they discover at the end of the hunt? Let's find out!

PIPPA
female plant hunter

NOAH
male plant hunter

MADDIE
female plant hunter

ANTWON
male plant hunter

JIN
male plant hunter

ANNABELLE
female plant hunter

ACT 1, SCENE 1

[**SETTING** *Near the entrance of City Botanical Gardens.*
MADDIE, JIN, ANTWON, NOAH, PIPPA, *and* ANNABELLE
are listening to MRS. BLANKENSHIP.]

MRS. BLANKENSHIP: Look carefully at your Scavenger
Hunt Notebook. Use it as much as possible. Be sure to wear
your gardening gloves because some plants are poisonous.
Have fun! I'll see you at the end for a *big surprise!*

[MRS. BLANKENSHIP *exits. Students look excited about
the big surprise.*]

NOAH: [*holds up Scavenger Hunt Notebook*] Let's look at
the notebook together. [*flips through pages and shows
group*] There is one page for each plant. We have to mark
"yes" or "no" for the plant **characteristics.** We also
have to list the plant name. There is room for our
comments, too.

PIPPA: Where do we begin?

ANTWON: [*pulls piece of folded paper out of pocket*] Mrs. Blankenship gave me this piece of paper when we came in. She told me not to look at it until the hunt started. Maybe it will help.

JIN: Will you read it to us?

ANTWON: It says, "I have a trunk. I stand tall. I'm named after one of the biggest animals of all."

ANNABELLE: [*confused*] That sounds like an elephant! [*excited*] Wait! I saw a big plant that had leaves like elephant ears when we came in.

MADDIE: Let's start there!

SCENE 2

[**SETTING** *All students walk to a tall plant in the corner. The plant has large, broad leaves. The leaves look like elephant ears.*]

JIN: You are right, Annabelle. These leaves sure do look like elephant ears! What a strange **adaptation.**

ANNABELLE: [*points to sign next to plant*] I was right. The plant's name is elephant ears!

NOAH: I'll write that down in the notebook. [*checks off characteristics while studying plant*] This plant has leaves, but I don't see any flowers.

MADDIE: [*measuring a leaf with measuring tape*] This leaf is 74 centimeters wide. It's 107 centimeters tall. It's huge! Let's write that in the comments section.

JIN: No flowers are

  blooming on this plant. It doesn't have vines or

  a scent. Check "no" for those characteristics.

PIPPA: We figured out this plant quickly. But

  where do we go next? Antwon, did Mrs. Blankenship

  give you any other clues?

ANTWON: [*holds up clue*] No, this is the only one.

ANNABELLE: Look! [*points to bottom of plant*] There is

  a new piece of paper!

NOAH: [*reads paper aloud*] "I'm tiny as can be. I'm an

  itty bitty tree!"

MADDIE: Let's go look for the new plant!

SCENE 3

[**SETTING** *Students are walking along the pathway.*]

PIPPA: [*thinking hard*] There are a bunch of trees in this habitat. Which one is the clue talking about?

JIN: [*points to nearby plant*] That plant over there looks like a tiny tree.

NOAH: I think you found it! This one is called a bonsai tree. [*writes name in notebook*]

PIPPA: The sign says this plant comes from Japan.

MADDIE: That's amazing! It also has small, pink flowers. [*sniffs*] They have a light scent. [*measures plant*] This plant is only 13 centimeters tall.

[NOAH *records characteristics in notebook.*]

ANNABELLE: It really does look like a tiny tree. We should write that in the comments section.

NOAH: [*writing*] No problem!

[JIN *reaches down. He pulls a piece of paper from under the plant's pot.*]

JIN: I found the new clue! "We do not sit on the ground. Look up high and think of *sound.*"

[*Students go to search for next plant.*]

SCENE 4

[**SETTING** *Students are looking at plants that are hanging from the ceiling.*]

NOAH: What kind of musical instruments do we know?

JIN: There's the flute, the saxophone, the violin, the guitar…

ANTWON: [*stops to read a plant name*] I found it! It's called angel's trumpet!

ANNABELLE: Those flowers do look kind of like trumpets. They are beautiful.

MADDIE: [*stretches to measure*] Wow—this plant is 2 meters tall! [*sniffs flowers*] The flowers smell great!

PIPPA: Be careful, Maddie. The sign says this plant is poisonous.

JIN: I'm really happy Mrs. Blankenship gave us these gloves!

[*All students nod and agree with* JIN.]

NOAH: I wrote down the information we need. Who has the next clue?

ANNABELLE: [*pulls clue out of middle of plant*] Here it is! It says: "I make many things taste yummy. Look up high where it's sunny."

ANTWON: [*excited*] I know that one right away! It's a vanilla orchid!

PIPPA: [*doubtful*] How do you know that?

ANTWON: My aunt grows orchids. She told me about the vanilla one. It's a huge vine. [*points to distance*] There it is!

[*Students walk to huge vine growing up a post.*]

PIPPA: I'm sorry I didn't believe you, Antwon. This sign says vanilla orchid. It says all of the vanilla in the world comes from these plants. The sign says they're originally from present-day Mexico.

NOAH: I'm going to write that along with our information. [*begins writing*]

MADDIE: [*looks worried*] Oh, no! I'm never going to be able to measure it. It's so high!

JIN: Let's **estimate** the height. I'm sure Mrs. Blankenship will understand. She wouldn't want us to climb up there!

ANNABELLE: I would estimate that it's about 5 meters tall.

[*Students nod in agreement. NOAH records information.*]

PIPPA: [*sniffs and makes a face*] Do you guys smell something? It stinks!

NOAH: [*sniffs orchid*] It's not this plant. This plant has a sweet scent. [*writes information in notebook*] It must be coming from something else.

JIN: [*pulls out piece of paper that is tucked in vine and reads it*] I think the final clue will help us. Listen to this: "Use your nose to find me. I don't smell like other lilies."

ANTWON: Follow that stinky scent!

29

SCENE 5

[**SETTING** *Students come around a corner.*
MRS. BLANKENSHIP is standing next to a gigantic plant. She
is holding her nose. NARRATOR enters and addresses audience.]

NARRATOR: The students are almost finished with
the Scavenger Hunt. They have recorded important
information about each plant they found. Now, they are
ready to find the big surprise—and boy, is it BIG!

MRS. BLANKENSHIP: Surprise! You made it!

[*Students make faces at stinky odor.*]

JIN: What is that?

MADDIE: [*quickly measuring*] It's 1.2 meters tall!

[NOAH *records information in the notebook.*]

MRS. BLANKENSHIP: [*laughing*] This plant is called the voodoo lily. It only blooms once a year. When it blooms, it smells like something is rotting! The scent attracts pollinators to help the plant reproduce.

NOAH: [*makes uncomfortable sound*] That's for sure. It smells awful!

ANNABELLE: [*interested*] I don't care that it smells bad. It's amazing! And it sure is a *big surprise.*

[*Students all nod in agreement.*]

MRS. BLANKENSHIP: [*happy*] I hope you had a good time today. You did a great job of identifying all of the plants. Would you like to come here again sometime?

[*Students all say "yes." They cheer.*]

Check In Which plant does vanilla come from?

Discuss Characters, Stories, and Main Ideas

1. What do you think connects the three pieces that you read in this book? What makes you think that?

2. Choose an illustration in "The King's Tree." What additional information does it give about the characters or the setting?

3. What is the main idea of "Extreme Plants"? Explain how you think each plant's most extreme feature might be useful to it.

4. In "The Plant Hunt," what event usually leads to the start of a new scene?

5. What do you still wonder about plants? What would be some good ways to find more information?